Myrna Mele

THE PICKET FENCE

Myrna Mele

Myrna Mele

DEDICATION

For my Mother
Her last name was Rose.
"Forever remembered in my heart"

The rose will hold the magic
Of the dreams I have for you
Its fragrance will still linger
Its beauty will still hold
And it will be remembered
Long after we've all grown old

—Myrna Mele

Myrna Mele

ACKNOWLEDGMENTS

This story was written in recognition of all the persons whom I have counseled through the grief process over many years. I wish to thank them for trusting me to help them through their loss and, in turn, for touching my heart as I hope this story touches yours.

My thanks to Carol Zimmerman (The von Raesfeld Agency, Henderson, NV) for helping me to get this story published.

I would also like to thank Dorothy Hardy for creating a perfect cover.

Myrna Mele

Dance in the meadows,

sing in the rain

For we will never walk in this

time and place again.

Myrna Mele

I

It was Christmas Eve and six year-old Allie was sitting in her room talking to her pet hamster, "Nibbles." Allie was telling the hamster about the trip she took with her Daddy to look for the end of the rainbow. That idea came to her one day when they were driving and Daddy asked her how far they should drive.

"To the end of the rainbow where we can find the pot of gold!" she said.

"We drove all the way to California! You know, Nibbles, we were going to go to Utah, but it was snowing there, so we drove to the farthest place we could think of. If you look for the end of the rainbow, it should be as far as you can drive 'cause it's a really big rainbow.

"Daddy asked me what I would do with the pot of gold if I found it. I told him that I would buy a whole bunch of donuts," she said, laughing.

As she talked about the fun she and Daddy had and the Christmas Eve she was looking forward to, she suddenly remembered that she didn't have a Christmas gift for Daddy. He was the one who always made her days a little brighter with his stories and the fun things he planned for them to do together. Nibbles was busy running up and down her arms and had just settled into a soft little ball of fur in her lap.

Just then, Allie heard three light taps on her bedroom door. It slowly opened and she turned her head to see who was there. Her Grammy tiptoed into her room all dressed up like Mrs. Santa Claus!

Grammy held her finger up to her lips to let Allie know to be very, very quiet. "Daddy is taking a nap and Mommy is baking your favorite chocolate chip cookies."

Allie whispered to Grammy, "I don't have a present for Daddy and it's Christmas Eve! Grammy, what can I give him?" she cried. Her soft brown eyes glistened with tears.

"Well," Grammy replied, "I've always thought that the best gifts we can give are the ones we make ourselves. That's because we take the time to make them with all the love that we hold in our hearts for that person. That love is a magical thing that lasts year after year."

Allie thought for a little while and then whispered, "Do you mean like the picket fence that Daddy made for me around my play yard?"

"Oh yes!" Grammy said, her eyes sparkling with happiness. "That was a wonderful gift that Daddy took many hours to make for you. Didn't it make you feel special and loved, just like Daddy wrapping his big arms around you real tight?"

"Oh yes, Grammy! It makes me feel really safe when I play there! It's like Daddy is always with me, even when he's not." Allie answered.

"He was always planting rose bushes in all the colors of the rainbow while I played," she said. "I really love them, especially the white ones! Daddy says they're called 'tea roses.'

Isn't that a funny name, Grammy? He told me that each rose's color has a special meaning. If you give someone a white one, it means they will always remember you. I will always remember Daddy and that's why I love them so!"

Suddenly, she jumped up. "I know what I can give Daddy and he will love it! Grammy, will you help me, please? I can do it by myself, but I need you to help me to carry some cans!"

She whispered to Grammy what her present was going to be and off they went to create his Christmas gift.

As they headed out the back door, her mother asked, "Where are you going? Don't you know it's really cold out there?"

Grammy said, "Don't worry, we'll be back soon. Allie and I are going to make some memories."

* * * *

The next morning, Allie awoke to the smell of her favorite homemade cinnamon rolls and her mother's yummy buttermilk pancakes. She jumped out of bed, pulled on her clothes and hurried down the stairs.

As she rounded the spiral staircase, she could see the Christmas tree and all of the colorful presents piled around it. Mommy, Daddy, Grammy, and Grandpa were all there waiting for her. They seemed puzzled at her reaction as she stood there looking at the tree and not moving.

"Allie, are you okay?" her mother asked.

Daddy took her hand. "Honey, Santa came last night. Aren't you excited?"

Allie smiled. "Oh yes, but I have a special surprise for you, Daddy. I want you to see mine first!"

She ran to get her coat and hat from the closet.

Mommy, Grammy, and Grandpa smiled and said, "That sounds like a great idea. Can we come too?"

"Sure!" Allie said. "I want all of you to see my present for Daddy!"

* * * *

Everyone put on their hats and coats and followed Allie outside through the snow to her play yard. Daddy seemed puzzled, but followed along with the others. When they got to the play yard, Allie took her daddy's hand and led him to the play area inside the picket fence.

"Grammy says that the best gifts are the ones you make yourself. That way, the magic of Christmas comes from inside your heart. You made the picket fence with roses all around it for me, so I decided to make something special just for you."

Allie ran to the picket fence and pulled the bright red blanket from it.

"Merry Christmas, Daddy!" she said as she showed him her gift. There on the inside of the fence was printed in her childish scrawl in all the colors of the rainbow...

"See Daddy, now the magic of Christmas will always be with you and so will I! And since we didn't find the end of the rainbow, I painted all of the rainbow colors here for you in your present!" she said.

"Oh Allie, that's the best gift I've ever received!" said her father as his eyes filled with tears. "Thank you for taking the time to paint it for me!"

Mommy, Grammy, and Grandpa looked very happy as Allie and Daddy shared a great big hug.

II

The years flew by as if on wings. Allie grew to be a fine young lady full of hopes and dreams of her own. With her father by her side, cheering her on, she felt as if anything she wished for could be hers if only she worked really hard.

Allie decided to become a nurse. She went to school to learn how to become one. Her father watched as she struggled to achieve her goal. He was her strongest supporter and through the years of training, he was always there for her.

On her graduation day, he sat in the front row of the auditorium with Mother, Grammy, and Grandpa right beside him.

* * * *

One day, Allie met a very special young man and fell in love. Her parents attended her wedding, but sadly her mother died a couple of years later.

A few years after that, Allie had two children of her own to love and care for. Her father was very happy to be a grandfather and to share his wisdom with them.

* * * *

Allie and her family moved to another state where she and her husband found jobs. Allie didn't get to see her dad as often as she wanted, but each time they visited him, her father played with his grandchildren inside the picket fence. He made sure to always remind them about the message their mother painted on the fence so long ago. He wanted them to know that it's not how much a gift costs, but the love and thoughtfulness that goes into making it that matters most.

Although Allie didn't know it, her father took a photograph of the fence to preserve the memory of her message. He never painted over her message. Through the years, the storms brought torrential rains that pounded hard upon the fence, the winds blew strong and snow piled high all around the picket fence, but still the fence stood. The colors had faded, but the words remained visible for all to see.

Myrna Mele

III

Allie's 40th birthday was coming soon. She wanted very much to visit her father again. She'd packed everything days ahead and planned to take the children with her so they could spend time with him. The tickets were purchased. Everything was ready for their departure on Friday.

On Wednesday, Allie had just returned home after grocery shopping. She wanted to be sure her husband would have plenty to eat while she and the children were gone. She turned to open the refrigerator door when she heard the phone ringing. She hurried to pick it up, cheerfully saying, "Hello."

At first there was silence on the other end and then she heard her Aunt Marie's voice saying, "I hate to give you this news, Allie, but your dear father passed away in his sleep last night."

Allie felt that time stopped in that moment. It was as if her heart had stopped beating and she could no longer breathe. *How could this be? I was going to see him in two more days! Why couldn't he wait for me?*

The world seemed to be spinning around and then she slowly sank to the floor in a state of shock. She had no tears to shed. It was as if everything had dried up inside of her.

* * *

After her father died, the days turned into weeks and the weeks into months. Allie felt like she couldn't lose one more thing without losing some part of herself. She felt like a robot following her daily routine—walking, talking, eating, and sleeping, but feeling no emotions.

Allie knew that her father would want her to move forward with her life. To do that she knew she had to go back to the home where she grew up and finish the task her father asked her to do. She was the executor of his estate, the person who carries out the wishes he'd written in his Will.

* * * *

Allie arrived at her father's home late in the afternoon. Standing there in the front yard, she thought of all the people she loved most who were no longer with her. She wandered out to her old play yard inside the picket fence and sat on the wooden swing her father had built for her many years ago. With each push of the swing, she remembered the exhilarating feeling as her feet reached for the blue sky overhead. It seemed as if they could touch the puffy, snow white clouds. She could almost feel her father standing behind her. The message she had painted on the picket fence that she wrote so many years ago was still visible. Tears fell like raindrops rolling down her cheeks like endless, salty streams of sorrow.

Her sobs went unheard. Her heart ached. The emptiness she felt could not be filled. She stopped swinging and slid to the ground, tucking her legs underneath her. She wrapped her arms around herself and cried for a very long time.

She wasn't sure how long she had been sitting there, wrapped up in her childhood memories when she heard the noise of a truck rumbling down the lane toward her father's house. *Who would be coming to see my father today?* she wondered.

As the truck got closer, she could see the words "Aerial Concepts" painted on the side of the truck. *That's strange,* she thought. *I'm not interested in listening to any sales people today!*

Allie remembered her father's cheerful attitude toward strangers and she dutifully walked toward the truck. She wiped her tears on the sleeve of her old blue sweater as she got closer to the visitor.

The driver got out of the truck holding a large package wrapped in brown paper.

"Excuse me, Miss, but is Mr. Henderson here?"

Allie looked at him. Her eyes glistened with tears. "I'm sorry to tell you this, but Mr. Henderson passed away two days ago."

A look of concern appeared on the man's face. "I am truly sorry for your loss. He seemed like such a kind, caring person. This package was supposed to be a birthday gift for his daughter, Allie. He said she was arriving for a visit this week and he wanted to be sure it was delivered on time to give to her."

Allie felt her throat tighten as she struggled with the emotions she felt. "I'm his daughter and today is my birthday!" She took the package and thanked him for it. She could feel the hot tears brimming in her eyes again as she thought of her father's thoughtfulness. He always remembered her special day. She thanked the man as he left and carefully carried the package over to the front porch.

She sat down in her father's favorite rocking chair and unwrapped the package, knowing this would be the last gift she would receive from him.

The little card tied to the ribbon read, "Forever Remembered! Love, Dad."

She carefully lifted the lid from the box and separated the layers of white tissue paper inside. Tucked within the tissue, she found a large, black-framed aerial photo. It was a full 12 x 16-inch color photo of her picket fence and play yard surrounded by her father's beautiful, colorful rose bushes.

What a wonderful photograph! she thought. She knew that she would always treasure this last gift from her father that held so many of her childhood memories in it.

As she gazed at the photo, her eye was drawn to the rainbow of colors of the rose bushes her father had planted around her picket fence. She remembered how he had spent many hours weeding and tenderly caring for them. They were planted so that they formed a rainbow arch that covered her playground area from one end to the other. The view was breathtaking from above!

Staring at the photo, engrossed in her memories of the past, she noticed that he had planted her favorite white roses in only one area near the end of the rainbow of roses.

She held the picture at arm's length, looking at it from different angles, turning it around and around.

She jumped to her feet when she saw it. Her father's special message to her was in the roses. He had planted green shrubs among the white roses that when seen from the aerial view, spelled what he knew she would understand and remember.

"Rainbow's End"
Love, Dad.

Although she could not see him, she knew he was there by her side once more.

Remember Me As I Remember You

The little girl twirls and as she spins
The years sweep by below the bright blue sky.
The magic tucked inside is lost to the
Undiscerning eye.

The cold winds blow
Bringing mounds of pure white snow.
Raindrops pound hard upon the picket fence
Paint fades, but memories live on
For a part of me, what is near and
Dear to my heart
Can never fade away
When I remember you.

—Myrna Mele

Myrna Mele

A SPECIAL THANK YOU

I want to say a special "thank you" to
my beautiful grandchildren,
Hallie and Anthony.
You are a constant source of
inspiration in my life.
You are truly a gift from God
and worthy of white roses always.

Myrna Mele

ABOUT THE AUTHOR

Myrna Mele is an Advanced Practice R.N. in Psychiatry and a published author. She currently lives in North Carolina with her husband, two sons, two daughters-in-law, and three grand-children. A third son and daughter-in-law reside in Ohio where she was born and raised.

She began her writing with poetry following the loss of her father and a crisis in her own life which kept her from her career for several months. Poetry became an avenue for the expression of thoughts and feelings not otherwise shared—a walk down memory lane where the laughter rings out and the smiles continue on.

The Picket Fence is a touching story about the close bond that exists between a father and his daughter. It takes the reader on a journey through the grief and loss that we all experience at some time in our lives. The picket fence represents a memory of the past that time cannot erase. It will stir the hearts and memories of parents and children everywhere.

OTHER BOOKS BY THIS AUTHOR

The Antique Toy is a story based on true happenings in the author's life. It describes a simpler time when families were bound together by love and experiences shared, a time when heroes lived and worked beside us and stood up for the values and beliefs they were taught as children.

It also reveals the healing magic that exists inside the toy, a magic that will remain forever in your heart.

AVAILABLE ONLINE!

Softcover and Kindle ebook:
www.amazon.com/books/

Softcover:
www.createspace.com/4562295

Softcover and Nook ebook:
www.barnesandnoble.com

Myrna Mele